Laugh out Loud!
Babies
By Sharon Irish

Laugh out Loud! Babies
Copyright: Sharon Irish

ISBN: 978-0-9926375-7-6
Published: 4th November 2013

Publisher: Sharon Irish

Cover by: Sharon Irish

Firstly, a little bit about this book:-

My first book, Laugh Out Loud! Pregnancy dealt with embarrassing and funny moments from Pregnant Women, but the laughs don't end when the baby has been born. This book proves it by sharing experiences and funny moments from Parents, family members and friends who are present during labour and after the baby makes an appearance.

You may not think that being in labour can have a funny side, but when you add pain relief into the mix we Ladies can say and do some very strange things when we are 'under the influence' which can be hilarious for the other people present!

When we bring the baby home it can be a completely new experience, we learn along the way how to deal with our new addition – usually by our mistakes, especially when we are sleep deprived, the brain just can't cope sometimes and we get ourselves into some situations which others find hilarious, even if we don't!

I really hope you enjoy reading this book, and these stories give you something to giggle at, maybe even laugh out loud!

Sharon Irish

Laugh Out Loud!
Babies

Labour and Birth:-………………………………………………9

Doctor's appointments and check-ups:-………………37

Feeding:-……………………………………………………….41

Nappy changing, poo and sick:-……………………….49

Siblings and other Children:-………………………….59

First words:-……………………………………………………..67

Other incidents:-…………………………………………………71

Labour and Birth:-

You've managed to get through all the embarrassing accidents you had during your pregnancy and you are so close to the end of it, just the labour bit to go, pretty straight forward right? Wrong!
Some of these has me literally rolling on the floor laughing:-

When I went into labour I was really controlled until it came to the emergency C section, then I was quite hysterical, the Anaesthetist had really bad breath and was right in my face explaining things to me and in my drugged up, hysterical state I thought I whispered to my Husband "Get her away from me, she stinks!" but I actually shouted it at the top of my lungs over and over again apparently, oops!
Melanie, UK

On the way to hospital in hard labour I was leaning out of the window, shouting "Get out the way! I'm having a

baby!" to all the cars in our way, then we went past
McDonalds and I was crying because we did not have time
to stop there as, obviously, I was about to have a baby!
Catherine, UK

Gas and Air had a peculiar effect on me. I had a case of
'talking with no control'. I was very aware of what I was
saying, but I couldn't stop myself from saying it! I said the
following:-
Midwife: "You need to push."
Me: "I can't."
Midwife: "Why not?"
Me: "I can't stop thinking about Johnny Depp."
My Partner: "Oh thanks, that makes me feel *really* good
about myself."
(I wasn't thinking about Johnny Depp, so I really don't
know why I even said that!)
Elaine, UK

I had only been at the hospital for two hours and the
Nurse had just checked me and I was five centimetres
dilated and feeling great. About fifteen minutes later, I
started feeling really bad and screaming that I needed to
push. I was really upset and screaming at everyone so the
Nurse finally came in and said that it hadn't been long
enough and she wasn't going to check me. I don't
remember but I guess I looked at my Husband right in
front of her and said "This Nurse is the stupidest b****
ever." Well I guess she looked horrified and decided to
check me and just as she did, my water exploded all over
her arm and I looked at my Husband and said "She
deserved that" (oops). She said that I was ten centimetres

dilated and the baby was coming, but she told me not to push because my Midwife wasn't there. So I was screaming "How am I not supposed to push?" My Midwife walked in then. Well I pushed once and the baby's head popped out and I started screaming to my Midwife "Put her back in! It hurts so bad please just put her back in!" Well obviously she didn't but my Husband still laughs about it and constantly reminds me.
Kelly, USA

I had gas and air and my Husband told me I started talking in an Irish accent to all the Midwives instead of my normal accent, random!
Jay, UK

I remember right before the baby came out the Doctor stepped away to put on a more protective jacket and I said something like, "Hurry the f*** up! There's a baby hanging out of my vagina!" The Doctor said to wait until the next contraction to push and I replied, "Well where the f*** is it?" That got the Nurses laughing but I was not at all amused at the time!
Susie, UK

Once I'd had an epidural and was lying on the bed (still sucking down the gas and air too!), the Midwife told me to let the pressure build as the baby was still too high up. I kept giggling and started whispering to hubby "This baby is trying to come out of my bum!" I said it so many times until the Midwife, who was laughing her head off, said "Honestly, it's really not."

Vicky, UK

When my Son's head started crowning, the Midwife said, "Oh that's really good, keep going, we can see the head" to which I cried out "Is it ginger?"
My Husband responded, "I can't tell, it's covered in blood!"
Emma, UK

While I was high on gas and air, the Midwife asked if she could examine me. I must have nodded or something but as soon as she put her fingers inside me, I shot into an upright position, looked her in the eye and screamed "GET YOUR F***ING HAND OUT OF MY FANNY RIGHT NOW!" My Husband was mortified. The poor Midwife shot across to the other side of the room and just said very quietly, "When you feel like you're ready to push, can you please let me know." The poor woman, I think she thought I was going to throttle her.
Amy, UK

I flirted outrageously with the Anesthetist when he came to do my epidural. His assistant numbed my back with this freezing spray which was amazing as it was so hot outside and I told him I loved him several times. My Husband was so embarrassed and told me to stop to which I replied "I will not! He has drugs, do you?"
Gillian, UK

When the really cute Doctor was stitching me up after birth, I was sucking away on the gas and air and decided to ask for an extra stitch to make me a virgin again. Needless to say he burst out laughing!
May, UK

I had torn quite badly when giving birth and while getting stitched up afterwards, I was still on the gas and air. The Doctor said she had to put a finger up my bum to check for damage up there and I said (high as a kite) "It's ok, I've had worse up there!"
Caroline, UK

During the last stages of labour with my first baby, the Doctor was leaning in closer for a better look just as I got a massive urge to push. Good job he was wearing goggles because at the same moment the most forceful projectile-pee jetted out of me at about a hundred miles an hour, hitting him right in his face!
My Husband still teases me about what pressure I managed to get up! I was like one of those games at the fair where you have to squirt down targets with a power-jet of water. He said I'd definitely have won a cuddly toy for that attempt!
Shelley, UK

When I delivered my Son I was really loopy on the hospital drugs and my labor went so fast they didn't have time to give me an epidural the 'correct' way and they had to administer it differently, I'm not sure how but the

Anesthesiologist came in and told me "This is Ann, Ann is going to be your best friend."
I looked at my Doctor and I said "No, the epiduural is my besh friend, then Ann." Those aren't typo's I was literally slurring my words!
Jamie, USA

I proudly announced to the whole room that my waters had gone only to be told I'd in fact done a massive wee, all over the bed!
Rachel, UK

During my labour with my Son they swapped staff and the new Midwife came in and introduced herself. All I could think about was that she looked like a horse. I kept thinking, "She has a horse face," and telling myself "Don't say it out loud, don't say it out loud." I thought she left the room and shouted "Oh my God she well looks like a horse!" It turned out she was still in the room! You've got to love gas and air!
Nicola, UK

When in labour with my Daughter they wheeled my bed through to labour and delivery, and I was moaning that I was hungry. My Midwife asked the Nurse who helped wheel me through if she could get me a sandwich, she huffed as if to say "That's not my job!" and said "There's only egg there."
I said "Oh that's fine" meanwhile I start on the gas and air. I started shouting "Where's that Woman with my bloody egg sandwich?" Then I phoned my friend and

asked her if she knew where the b***h was who was supposed to be getting my egg sandwich! Then I phoned my Mum and whined "Muuuuuum can you make me an egg sandwich?"
The next day I'd totally forgotten about it and my friend wrote on my Facebook wall "Want an egg sandwich?" Ha Ha!
Ashley, UK

In the throes of labour and high on gas and air, I looked at my Husband quite seriously and told him to ask John Travolta to get me a cold sprite from the machine!
Rebecca, UK

My Nurse had come into the room to change the pad underneath me because my water had just broken and I was so numb from the waist down I couldn't tell when I was going to fart. Sure enough she leaned over and I let out the loudest one ever right near her head! Never been so embarrassed in my life!
Keeley, USA

When the Midwife was checking me for tears after our little one was born, I said to her "Stop playing with my bits - it hurts!" I have no idea why I used the word 'playing' I blame the gas and air! But the best part was my Husband looked all offended and said "but I'm not even touching you!"
Madeline, UK

With my first Daughter I was induced and I'd been in hospital ages before they found room for me so I was tired. At the end I was pushing and the Midwife said "Wow, that's a lot of hair." Cue me apologising and saying I was too big myself but Hubby had tried to neaten me up before we came in.
Hubby pointed out that obviously she meant the baby's hair, as the Midwife practically rolled on the floor laughing *blush*!
Eve, UK

I had a dose of 'Stadol' a few hours before I had my epidural and boy, did it make me loopy! I kept telling my Husband and Sister, who were in the room with me that I had forgotten to breathe, and could they please perform CPR on me!
Josie, USA

When I was nearing the end of labour and I was pushing my Son out, I started to feel the head begin to come out. During a break while waiting for a contraction, I asked the Midwife "Will I feel his ears coming out? Like the actual texture of the ears rubbing over my vagina?" I wasn't nervous about it, just curious. She stared at me like she misheard and said that in 25 years of delivering babies, she'd never heard that question!
Marianne, UK

This is a conversation I had with the Midwife when I was in labour and on gas and air:-

Me: "I'm s****ing myself."
Midwife: "No you're not."
Me: "Yes I am, I can feel it."
Midwife: "Okay."
Me: "I'm not bothered, I'm just saying."
She looked at me like I was a weirdo!
Nicola, UK

When the Midwife checked me I was only 2-3cm dilated.
Thirty minutes passed and I thought I had made progress
so asked to be checked again. This time the Doctor
checked me and he said "No, you're still the same."
I said "Did you take into consideration that your hands are
bigger than hers?" He laughed, although I didn't find it
funny at the time.
Tina, UK

This is a bit strange, but when I was in labour I found that
I needed to dance in order to ease the pain. When the
Midwife walked in she saw me and my Husband doing the
tango while I was high on diamorphine! She said that she
had seen Women do many things during labour, but that
was the first time she had ever seen that!
 Layla, UK

During labour, my Sister got really hot, whipped off her
top, did a little wiggle and shouted "Woo! I'm naked! my
t**s are out!" She repeated this to everyone who was in
the room, but then five minutes later, she burst into tears
crying "Everyone has seen my boobs and they're your

boobs!" (to her Husband) I must point out that she was high on gas and air at the time!
Isla, UK

I was in labour and experiencing a lot of pain, waiting, and waiting for my pain relief. I felt like I couldn't take it any longer and said to my Husband "Where's that f***ing bitch with my pethadine?" I didn't realise she was on the other side of the room! Oops!
Lesley, UK

I had a home birth with my second child and I was in labour when two horrid Midwives came round. Half way through my labour I noticed that one of them was wearing really dodgy socks and kids school shoes. By this point I had used quite a lot of gas and air and I said (quietly, I thought) "Does she expect me to take her seriously when she's wearing those stupid f***ing socks and kids shoes?" My best mate who was my birthing Partner burst out laughing and didn't know where to put herself and the Midwife just looked up at me from her paperwork and gave me an evil look!
Joanna, UK

When I went into labor with my Son I was super excited but was sure I wasn't really in labor so when I went to the hospital to get checked and they started hooking me up and admitting me I realized that I really *was* in labor and I freaked out and said "I've changed my mind, I'm going home" and started gathering my stuff while my Mom sat there laughing at me. The Nurse came back in after

hearing me freak out and convinced me that the baby was coming out no matter where I was and said "We have drugs!" So I had my epidural and told my worried Husband "It feels like a cloud has been shoved up my ass!" Everyone asked what I said and he said "She feels like she's floating on a cloud."
I loudly corrected him "No, up my butt! The cloud is up my butt and its wonderful!"
Britney, USA

When it was time to push I insisted I had to fart. I begged everyone who walked near me to clear the room so I could fart. Of course they wouldn't and the Doctor got ready and clapped his hands and got into a Position like the football guys do when they catch the ball. I looked and him and sighed "Alright but I swear I'm just going to fart really loud so don't say I didn't warn you." He just laughed at me!
Grace, USA

When the Doc told me to start my first push, I knew you were supposed to push hard but I pushed so hard that a stream of goo shot out of me and hit my Husband right in the face! He said later than he should have known better than to stand at that end!
Kaitlyn, USA

During labour I was standing at the foot of the bed, rocking my hips back and forth and I kept having this clear fluid dribble out of me. I couldn't understand how my water kept on coming out. My kind Mother then informed

me that it wasn't my water, I just kept peeing on the floor! So embarrassing!
Holly, UK

By the time I got to the hospital I was so far along that I was taken straight to the delivery ward and given gas and air. I was insanely hot and asked if I could strip down to my bra, but the old hag of a Midwife was weird about it and made me feel like it was inappropriate. So after a good few puffs on the gas and air I started telling her "You are the meanest Woman I've ever met, why are you doing this job if you're just going to make everyone feel like crap?" Then as the effects of the gas and air wore off between contractions I proceeded to apologise for saying that and said "I'm sure you're not a horrible person, I just think you could be a bit more tactful." Then I got another contraction and took some more gas and air, and finished my sentence with "Instead of acting like a total bitch!" At which point she said "I'll come back and check on you in a few minutes" and I started begging her not to go and saying "I didn't mean it!"
Lisa, UK

After I had given birth I had two Doctors stitching me up and I was told to keep the gas and air. I was puffing away on it, telling the Doctors that I wished I could see into my vagina to admire their work and that I was sure it looked beautiful! (I'm so glad I couldn't see!) I was asking what kind of stiches they were doing and whether they enjoyed this part of their work?! Oh how embarrassed I was when the gas and air wore off!
Jess, UK

When I was about to give birth to my twins the Doctor said "We might have to do an emergency C-section." I replied "I'll push 'em out thank you very much!" A few hours later my Brother in Law had come to see them and said "Wow they're so small, especially this little fella. I said very angrily "No they are not, they're ginormous!" No one dared to mention it again for the rest of visiting time!
Amanda, UK

During my really long labor my Mother in Law was there and I remember turning to her and telling her to go get something to eat because she hadn't eaten since dinner the previous night. She then said something like, "I don't want to make you feel hungry."
I replied "Look Woman, I could really care less about food right now. I'm more concerned about having to push this baby out of my vagina!" My Doula thought this was hilarious and proceeded to post it on Facebook!
Andrea, USA

Between pushing I was puffing away on the gas and air, I was high as a kite! The Midwife told me to push and I refused, looked at my wrist (with no watch on) and said "Sorry but it's my coffee break now." My Husband was doubled over laughing and the student Midwife walked out of the room holding her hand over her mouth, I didn't see what their problem was, I only wanted a coffee. Ha Ha!
Claire, UK

I'd had a spinal block because I needed forceps and so couldn't feel anything from the waist down after they had done it. After my Son was born and they were busy wrapping him up and checking him I was looking around and saw some large blue things in the air. I asked my Husband what they were, and with a very straight face he said, "They're your legs."
Kerry, UK

The Doctor gave me some extra pain relief through the epidural tubing that made me say crazy things. I could hear myself talking but just could not control it. The Nurses were laughing most of the time in between contractions and pushes. Some of the things I remember saying were "Just so you know, I'm not opposed to a lot of stitches. I'd like one of those designer celebrity vaginas." Then after a really bad contraction a moment later I said "Ok, just tell the Doctor to sew it shut please. We are done having children." Then when they said they could see the head, I asked "Is it very fuzzy?"
Brianne, USA

I didn't know I had an embarrassing story until I got up the nerve to watch the video of my Son's birth. I remember as I was pushing my hip cramped up and I needed to put my legs down on something, so I lowered my leg and relaxed for a minute. Right after that a Nurse grabbed my foot and I thought, "Oh thank goodness, what a helpful Nurse."
As I watched the tape I saw that I had rested my foot right

on the Doctor's face! The Nurses and Doctor started laughing and the Nurse quickly grabbed my foot. Luckily the Doctor had a sense of humor!
Amber, USA

When I was in labour, the Doctor kept coming in to check on my progress. I had been given gas and air, but I could still feel what he was doing and I told him to stop checking me because of his 'sausage fingers.' My Husband looked shamed and went bright red. At the time though I couldn't have cared less!
Katrina, UK

I had a horribly long labour. At one point I turned to my Husband and said "Get that dog out of here! I don't want her (my friend) or him (her dog) anywhere near me!' My Husband as calmly as he could said "Erm, you're in hospital?"
When the baby finally started to crown after hours of pushing, the Midwife said, "There's the head coming, do you want to feel it?" to which I growled "I *can* f***ing feel it!" though of course she meant with my hand. I was so traumatised by the time the baby was born that when they put him on me right after I just given birth, I shouted "Oh my God! It's a baby! Get it off me!" The poor baby!
Jackie, UK

When I was at the pushing stage the Midwife kept telling me to 'get angry' with my contractions, to which I replied "Please, kindly shut the f**k up." I was on gas and air which had started to make me feel sick but my Husband

tried to give it back to me and said "Take this, it will make you feel better."
I threw it at his head and told him "I don't f***ing want it." When giving me stitches afterwards the Midwife said "Focus on your baby and you won't feel a thing." Two stitches in and I virtually screamed "You b***h! you lied to me! I can feel every one of those f***kers going in!" I apologised later and felt awful. I don't normally swear either, my Husband was mortified!
Melanie, UK

During Labour my Mum was offering me lip balm as my lips were dry, I replied with "I couldn't care less about *those* lips, it's my *other* lips I'm concerned about!" Ha Ha! I was so embarrassed later, and it didn't help that she kept repeating it to everyone!
Susan, UK

I needed to go to theatre as my little one needed some help coming out. After two lots of morphine and a good whack of gas and air they gave me the spinal. They put my legs up in the stirrups, which is when I said in front of a team of about ten medical staff "Erm, excuse me, sorry to bother you, but can I just ask, whose legs are those?" (Pointing at my legs of course) Cue the whole room laughing at me and me not understanding what was so funny!
Angela, UK

I had been in labour for around 50 hours (not exaggerating!) and I had been on gas and air for quite a

while. I was begging my Husband to make it stop, then I told him I was on a secret mission and he had to go and buy some Christmas trees! It was May!
Gemma, UK

During my labour I had a Midwife and a trainee Midwife in with me. The poor trainee, I was her first and I don't think she will ever forget it!
I was given gas and air, but after the first puff I didn't like it so would not take any more. Every time I had a contraction the trainee would tell me to suck on the gas and air and I got so mad at her I threw the mouthpiece at her and said "You suck on it!"
She then moved my fan and I stopped mid push and shouted "And what do you think you are doing with that?" Poor girl, she looked at me as if I had threatened to kill her!
Carmen, UK

I had gas and air during my labour and was still feeling the effects when my little man was born. They put him in my arms and the first thing I said was "Eww it's all slimy! Take it away!"
Esther, UK

I was in established labour and in a lot of pain when we arrived in the delivery suite. The Midwife asked my Husband to go back to our previous room and get the CTG monitor. When I realised he was gone I asked where he was and when she told me I replied "If he's gone for a

f***ing fag I want a divorce!"
Kayla, UK

I used an all-female clinic because I didn't want any male medical staff involved with my labour. When I got to the hospital, 6cm dilated and in so much pain, I was admitted to triage where hospital staff examine you and decide whether to admit you to labour and delivery. The young student Doctor on duty walked in to examine me and in the middle of a contraction I took one look at him and yelled "Oh f**k, it's a dude!" Apparently everyone resisted the urge to burst out laughing.

I was also dubbed 'the screamer'. One of the Nurses asked me to keep it down because I was scaring the other patients. I apparently screamed back "Do I look like I give a f**k about them?" and carried on breaking noise code levels!

When I was pushing, the Nurse asked me if I wanted to see as it would make me realise what kind of push was working. She put a mirror between my legs and said "Look, see, she has a head full of hair, do you see her?" I replied "No, I can't tell the difference but I guess that's what I get for not having a bikini wax in nine months." The Nurse fell about laughing.

I can't remember doing any of these things! I'm usually very polite and never swear so it seems like labour brought out a different side of me!
Julie, UK

I loved gas and air during my labour, I was like a woman possessed with it. It was the best high ever and no-one was taking it off me. Some tried and failed. It didn't make me sick either which was a bonus. I was in labour for ages but the gas and air made me feel like I was on one exciting adventure trip. My Mother was there and I kept offering it to her saying "You gotta try this s**t Mum, it's unreal!" and when the Midwife tried to take it off me I yelled "Don't you take my air! I need it to breathe! It makes me f***ing high!" It did make me so calm during the contractions. I ended up having an epidural to give birth so couldn't feel a thing. When the Doctor told me to push I just said "What do I push? I can't feel anything down there! Okay I'll pretend I'm having a s**t, maybe that will work?" My Mother looked like she wanted the ground to swallow her up!
Alison, UK

My epidural didn't work on my left side and it was the middle of the night and I couldn't sleep, and my Husband was asleep in the recliner beside me. I am severely addicted to 'Chapstick' and the most horrible thing happened. I dropped it and it rolled away.
I woke up my Husband and this is how the conversation went:-
Me: "I dropped my Chapstick. I really need it."
Him: *Begrudgingly gets up and looks around* "I can't find it."
Me: "Look harder!"
Him: *looks around some more* "I don't know where it is."
Me: "find it!"

Him: "I looked around, it's not here!"
Me: "It's here! I dropped it in this room! It is *still* in this room!"
Him: "I don't know what you want me to do!"
Me: "I am having the most painful contractions delivering this stupid baby you put inside me and I can't sleep, I am barfing, my hands won't stay still and I don't think it's too much to ask that you find my Chapstick! Get on your hands and knees and go over every inch of this floor until you find it!"

So he did and he found it. We laugh about it now but I was *so* annoyed at the time. I don't know what would have happened if he hadn't found it!
Sherri, USA

When my waters broke at thirty seven weeks with my third child, I woke my Husband, then went downstairs to the kitchen cupboard where I had a list of numbers, Midwife, Hospital etc. I dialed the number carefully (at 5am) and a Lady answered. I said "Hi I think my waters have just broken" (they didn't with previous labours.) The lady said "Pardon?" so I repeated myself. Then the lady replied "That's nice dear but I think you need to call the hospital." I had somehow managed to dial the wrong number and woken some poor woman from her sleep! I profusely apologised and then dialed the *right* number!
Helen, UK

I had too much gas and air and whenever everyone left the room I was hiding my notes or throwing things out of the window! They must have loved me. Apparently my

Husband came back at one point to find me in a plastic apron and gloves (found in the delivery suite) declaring I didn't need a Midwife, I would do it by myself.

I had the hormone drip and an epidural which failed. I had to lean forward off the side of the bed for it and my Husband had to hold me still but he moved and I fell off the bed just before the needle went in, smashing into one of those screens on wheels which flew across the room.

I apparently then asked my Midwife in a 'Joey from friends' manner "How *you* doin?" and went on to try and chat her up!
Joanne, UK

I still don't know why but gas and air had a really strange effect on me. Between contractions I was running round the room pretending to be a plane!
Janine, UK

With my second birth it was a planned C section but I went into labour early. Contractions were coming every three minutes and I was 5cm dilated. The Midwife came in and said there was a phone call for me, it was my Mum, and could I tell her to stop ringing the emergency line. I asked them what she wanted and the Midwife replied "She wants to know how to get the telly onto sky." I was so embarrassed and spent the whole of my surgery apologising again and again! I could have throttled her!
Abby, UK

I was meant to be having a home birth with my second Son. After being in the bath for 20 minutes, I called my Partner and told him the baby was going to fall out when I stood up to get out! (it did feel like that) He panicked and told me to stay there while he called the Midwife. In the Midwife came, and I had crawled to my bedroom from the bathroom and I was 8 cm's dilated but my waters had not broken so she called an ambulance. By the time I was in the ambulance I was grateful for the gas and air and greedily sucked 3/4 of the ambulance supply! The only problem with all that deep breathing of the gas and air was that the first thing I announced at the Hospital was (in a very deep voice) "They do know I'm not here for a sex change don't they?" My Partner couldn't stop laughing and assured me that they knew I was having a baby!
Rachel, UK

My Son measured large from the start of my pregnancy. Ultrasound estimates were 8lbs 8oz. Lying there during my C Section, I heard him cry, then they called out "He's 9-8!" A few minutes later I heard "9-9!" Not realizing it was his Apgar scores, I yelled, "OMG, He's still growing?"
Leona, UK

The funniest memory I have is that my Father in Law was alone in the waiting room for most of the night but stuck his head in the room to check on everyone right as my Daughter was crowning. At a loss for words in the situation he timidly asked "Anyone want a cup of tea?" and then ran back out! Ha Ha!
Jenny, UK

We had been driving to the Hospital for about five minutes and my Wife started screaming and shouting at me through a large contraction. Stupidly, I asked "Are you ok? Should I pull over?"
As the contraction eased she shouted "You've trapped my finger in the f***ing window you w***er!"
Neil, UK

My Husband refused to go to any birthing classes, wasn't interested in watching any videos or reading any books on labour, he was fine just 'winging it.' As it turned out he was a great birthing Partner, I have no complaints. But, He didn't know about the placenta. There he was, cooing and holding our baby girl, and the Doctor murmured to me to push again, and I pushed hard, which made it sort of fly out, along with lots of blood. My Husband jumped back in horror and cowered in a corner, he thought I was dying or something. He was pretty white-faced!
 Sarah, UK

When I was giving birth to my first, the Doctor told my Partner to look just as the baby's head was crowning. My Partner got this horrified expression on his face. He told me later that when he saw the head crowning, it was literally just the crown of the baby's head and (his words), he thought that was the full size of her head and that we were having a 'midget.'
Michelle, UK

Finally after getting to 8cm dilated (eight hours of labour) we got rushed to theatre due to baby's heart rate dropping. When they got him out with the forceps the Doctor didn't tell us if we had a boy or a girl and it was up to my Husband to tell me.

When he went over to the baby area all I heard rather loud was "Wow he has huge balls!" The Doctor stitching me up stopped stitching for a moment and laughed, then carried on, but the whole theatre went silent for a second. So I knew when he said that, that we had a boy!

I don't know what it is with Men, when my Husband was calling people about the birth of our Son, I heard this over and over again:

"He was born Tuesday morning. She's doing fine. We named him Ethan. He has huge balls!" Seriously, he went on like this for weeks!

Then a friend of ours had a Son, and we went to the hospital to visit them. We were talking about how much he weighed when he was born and stuff when the new Daddy said, "I am so proud! This kid has an enormous set of balls!" Seriously, he looked fit to burst with pride. Lori, USA

I had just given birth having had no drugs or epidural and was pushing out the placenta. I noticed that my Husband had a very shocked look on his face as the Doctor was pulling on the cord, the placenta slid out as I pushed and I cried out a bit as it hurt. Later on he told me that he thought the Doctor was pulling out my intestines and guts and he nearly passed out. I laughed so hard, then started crying because laughing made my very sore 'hoo-ha' throb in pain!
Julia, USA

I work as a Nurse in a Hospital and when a couple who didn't speak English came in, the Woman was ready to deliver. The Man kept trying to get out of the delivery room, but we kept insisting he had to stay for moral support. When the baby emerged, I turned the Man's head so his eyes were on the delivery. Unfortunately, the next day I found out that he wasn't the Woman's Husband. He was her Brother!
Mya, UK

I'm a Midwife and when I was at work once, a patient was having trouble pushing. Her belly was numb from the epidural so I told her to push hard enough so that she could feel it in her chest. I was demonstrating so intensely that I passed gas, really loudly! I told her, "See, if you push, things happen down there!" She laughed so hard that she ended up giving birth to her baby in hysterics.
Janet, UK

We had been told that the baby (via a scan) was a girl so we had little pink going home outfits and everything. When I pushed the baby out the Midwife said to me "Look down and see what you've got" So I sort of looked down but didn't really look properly as I was just catching my breath and she repeated it a bit more loudly so I looked again, my Son spread his legs and peed all over me. All I could was say was "Oh my god, there's a penis!" Everyone was just about peeing themselves laughing at me!
Jessica, UK

I was in labor with my Son, who is seventeen months old now, for what seemed a very long time. I couldn't have an epidural because I was too swollen and it would put me at risk of being paralyzed. I started contractions around 11:00am on a Tuesday and started pushing at around 9:00pm. The Doctor finally got him out at 7:00am the next morning. I remember asking her over and over to just cut him out but the funniest thing I said (and I can't believe I said it) was "Why can't we just lay eggs?" The Doctor stopped in her tracks as well as the Nurses and they just looked at each other and we all started laughing. The Doctor looked at me and said "I've never heard that one before!"
Tanya, USA

I was in labor with my third child, had just been checked and was only 3cms dilated. I had to use the restroom so I got up and waddled down the hall. Did my business and that was when my water broke. Right into the toilet. At first I had no idea what was going on, I just thought I couldn't stop peeing. It finally dawned on me what was going on after sitting there for the longest time gushing fluids. I had never had my water break so early and as soon as it did my labor became seriously intense.

Fast forward to finally getting a room. I asked the pain medicine Nurse if I could have some yet, and she smiled with it already in her hand. I started to feel whatever it was just about immediately. My Husband burst into laughter, as did the Nurse, when my eyes glazed over and I started singing very loudly "Born freeeeeee, free as the wind blows!"

Fast forward again, contractions were worse, meds had worn off, but I was still a little loopy and for some reason, no one could figure out how to keep the door shut to my room. People just walked in and out of it without ever thinking to shut it. At one point, a random Man walked by and saw me yelling and moaning in pain, quickly turned his head away, and that was when I realized my gown was open. I flipped. I yelled out to the Nurses and Midwives in the hall "Do you people think we are on a farm? Can't anyone figure out how to shut an f***ing door! I don't want random people walking by to see my angry vagina!"
Julia, USA

At the time I was horrified, now I giggle at this story. Just after our Son was born and the Doctor was fixing me up (I had to have stitches due to a second degree tear) He looked up from between the stirrups and said. "I have this bit of skin and I'm not sure what side it belongs to so I'm just going to cut it off." I was so shocked I couldn't speak, so I just nodded.
Rhonda, USA

During a contraction it suddenly occurred to me that I had gotten pregnant in mating season (my Husband is a dairy farmer) and I was now giving birth during calving season. This resulted is a major hysterical laughing fit which started my Husband and my Midwife off laughing. Then whilst having an internal my Midwife said "Mmmm, that's lovely" (meaning things were progressing well) Me, in my deranged state, again got the giggles and blurted out

"Well that's a first, I've never had a Woman between my legs say that before. Actually I've never had a Woman between my legs at all." My poor Midwife!
Janine, UK

Doctor's appointments and check-ups:-

Okay so you have got through labour and birth, and you now have your baby, but you need medical examinations and they don't always go smoothly or without incident, as you can tell by some of these stories:-

I had a third degree tear and had really bad, uncontrollable wind for a while. About three days after the birth the Midwife came round to check my stitches. I had to lie on my side and she lifted my bum cheek and, yep you guessed it, I trumped right in her face! I was mortified!
 Jennifer, UK

A couple days after I had my little girl I had a blood transfusion. My Sister was there and I was sleeping. Apparently (and I do remember this vaguely) a Nurse came in to change my line as I was sleeping and said "Can I please borrow your arm?"

I said in the most innocent sleepy voice "Ok but I might need it back later" My Sister will not let me live it down!
Laura, UK

About three hours after I had given birth, I had all sorts of visitors in my room. A Nurse came in and turned me on my side to 'check my bottom.' Everyone got really awkward and tried to look away and talk amongst themselves, however, when I got turned on my side I couldn't stop farting. They came like loud blasts one after the other. My epidural was still lingering so I had no muscle control and couldn't stop it and they just kept coming and coming. Everyone was trying to ignore it as they are all very proper, which really made it more awkward than if they had just laughed. So I was already just about dying of embarrassment from about ten farts in a row, but then the Nurse loudly exclaimed that I had given myself a hemorrhoid from pushing! The whole room just went silent and I could have slapped that Nurse!
Megan, UK

It was my postpartum checkup and at the time I was still breastfeeding. I had pumped before I went but the wait was so long that when I finally got into the room, my breasts were full again. Anyway, I was lying there in the nice little sheet thing waiting to be checked and the Doctor was getting ready to check my breasts and pulled back the sheet and my boobs just started squirting everywhere, even on his glasses and his face. It was the most embarrassing thing that has ever happened to me but was funny at the same time. The poor Doctor didn't

know what to do and I guess because I was in shock, I
started giggling and couldn't stop for a while!
Eva, USA

Feeding:-

There are moments in a first time Mum's life when she feels like her body is not her own, and one of those surely has to be when their milk comes in, it just feels so strange. It is hard to get used to milk constantly leaking from you like a tap whether you are breastfeeding or not, it's something you need to put up with, but not always something you are prepared for. Of course feeding doesn't just relate to milk, when you are beginning to feed your baby actual food, it can be an education!:-

I had only given birth to my Son about a week before and I was in the grocery store, food shopping when this lovely young lady came up to me and said "Aww did you just have a baby? (in the sweetest voice ever and I didn't have my newborn with me)
I said "Yeah, how'd you know?"
She replied (in a really loud, evil voice) "Because you're leaking!" and walked away! I was so embarrassed because I looked down and my whole shirt was soaked.

This was my first baby and so I had no idea that would happen, or that people could be so mean to a new Mom!
Chrissy, Maine, USA

When my Husband and I were ready to get physical again after our Daughter was born, he was really interested in my new full breasts. Well, as we were getting into things and I was on top of him, my breasts started spraying milk all over his chest and face. I had no idea that would happen! It was horrific and hilarious at the same time!
Kristen, USA

A couple of weeks after I gave birth to my Son I was breastfeeding him and as usual I was wearing those silly pads that slip into your bra so you don't leak onto your clothes. One day I was shopping with a friend and as I was approaching the checkout lane I felt some wetness around my boob area and low and behold, my breastfeeding pad had escaped and done a disappearing act. I was horrified and as I went to turn and look around me in shock, this male shop assistant who had to be 16-17 years old came up to me holding my breastfeeding pad and said "Mam I think you dropped this." Right at that moment I think it hit him, that he was holding what had dropped out of my bra and he hurried and gave it to me and pretty much ran from me in embarrassment. My friend was doubled over laughing and said "Well I don't know who looked more embarrassed, you or the poor kid!" I haven't shopped there since!
Marianne, USA

I didn't breastfeed my Son but he has an obsession with boobs! He loves pulling my top down and blowing raspberries on my chest or playing with my bra strap. One day we were at my Boyfriend's Grandma's and he tried pulling her top down to blow raspberries on *her* chest! Oh Dear! She did see the funnny side though.
Janet, UK

My Daughter is ten months old and has been exclusively breastfed since day one. I'm a stay at home Mom so I'm particularly used to just kind of whipping one out when needed all day. The other day she was extra fussy due to teething so I gave her some teething tablets and nursed her for comfort reasons. That was when the doorbell rang. Well, I plopped her on the floor to play, hopped up to answer the door and there is the UPS guy with some stuff I had ordered. It wasn't until I opened the second door and got hit with the 14 below temperature that I realized that my nursing bra was still down and my shirt was still up! I was totally flashing the mail guy! I have caught myself several times since she was born walking from one room to another before realizing I was still exposed!
Gill, USA

I was at the theatre with my Husband on a 'date' while Grandma minded the baby. All of a sudden my milk let down and my boobs got so big and hard I had to go to the bathroom, lean over the toilet and milk myself like a cow; one boob in each hand. I was praying no one came in! Ever since then my Husband has called me 'Moomy.'

Joanna, USA

I never cover up when I'm breastfeeding and on the bus one day my baby Daughter suddenly unlatched during a fit of giggles and I shot the window and the person in front of us with milk. I nearly peed from laughing so hard! The guy I shot thought it was pretty damn funny too, luckily. Lately she has been trying to talk while nursing which makes this kind of muffled sound. We get some strange looks, especially when we are out and about.
Kate, USA

I have tons of funny 'squirting milk' stories (I have breastfed all of my children) but I think the funniest was when my Daughter pulled herself off my breast whilst feeding and put her hand on my breast, causing the milk to squirt me in the eye. She thought it was so funny she did it again! Little monkey! Ha Ha.
Johanna, USA

My Daughter will pause feeding to blow very loud raspberries on me and giggle like it's the funniest thing she's ever done in her life. Sometimes she cannot get herself back under control so we have to take a break and come back to it later.
Debbie, UK

When our Daughter was about three months old, we were on a flight to visit my family. There was this very nice flight attendant on the plane who kept coming by to

smile at us and let us know that he'd be happy to warm up a bottle whenever we needed it and we shouldn't hesitate to ask. About the third or fourth time he offered, my Husband said, very cheerfully, "Thanks, but it's okay, we don't need bottles. We have a twenty four hour breastaurant!" The attendant tried to laugh it off but it was obvious he was really embarrassed!
Alison, USA

My hubby and I were sitting on the couch and our 9 month old had just finished nursing when she pulled back and, out of curiosity I guess, decided to 'tweak' my nipple with her little pincer grip. I looked down in surprise just in time to see her squirt herself in the eye! She jumped, I laughed, and my Hubby leaned over to see what was so funny. You guessed it....she squirted him too! I laughed so hard I cried!
Nicole, USA

My 4 year old Daughter and I were at a store last week with my 2 month old. We were in line and the baby started to cry. My Daughter said, really loudly "Mom, I think she wants your boobies" (I was breastfeeding). I just wanted to hide because the line was all Men who were clearly trying not to notice, but doing a really bad job of it!
Heidi, USA

My little one was at the stage where she wanted to eat by herself and one day we were in a lovely café. My Daughter had finished her lunch and so I have her a

yoghurt which she insisted on feeding herself, and would not let me go anywhere near her spoon. She was having a lovely time although she was making a terrible mess. At the point where I thought she was just messing around with it and not eating it anymore, I attempted to take the spoon off her, which happened to be full of yoghurt at the time. She saw what I was about to do and forcefully threw her arm upwards, away from me, propelling the yoghurt up and behind her – right into the face of the Man sitting on the table next to us! I was mortified, but my little one thought it was hilarious and was laughing at the top of her voice. Luckily for me the Man saw the funny side!
Tina, UK

When I weaned my Daughter off breast milk she was almost three, so she had an understanding of a lot of things. I tried to explain that Mommy's nipples were broken and so she couldn't use them for nursing anymore. My Daughter thought about this for a while and then left the room. When she returned she had the scotch tape, which we used to repair one of her books the week before. She held it up to me and asked if we could fix' my nipples with it.
Mandy, UK

My fifteen month old loves fruit and whilst shopping one day I was trying to distract her while I carried on shopping, so I gave her a container of strawberries to hold thinking she couldn't get into them, but trying to would keep her busy while she's sat in the cart. How wrong I was! Pretty soon an old Lady tapped me on the arm and

pointed out that she had not only got into the container but now she looked like a juice-covered squirrel, her cheeks bulging with strawberries! That taught me never to stop watching her, even for a minute!
Alexa, USA

When my Son was around two, we were out shopping and I asked him what vegetable he would like with his dinner. He started shouting "Bloccoli! Bloccoli!" so we picked a head of broccoli and I gave it to him to hold while I got a bag to put it in but before I could, he held it up to his face and took a huge bite out of it! People around us started laughing, amazed that one, a toddler would love broccoli so much and two, that he would eat it raw!
Jane, UK

Nappy changing, poo and sick:-

So the birth is over and its plain sailing from here (not!) Get ready for yet more embarrassment caused by your little bundle of joy. When my little boy was a tiny baby I often wondered how someone so small could create so much mess. Even so, nothing could make you love them any less:-

My Husband was changing our little one's nappy once and she had pooed. He thought he caught it in the nappy. He put his hand down and she had actually pooed into his hand! I almost peed myself laughing and he was running about trying not to be sick!
Sophie, UK

The baby was having a nappy change and it was my Boyfriend's turn to do it. She had only done a pee, so he thought he had an easy one. He was just getting the new nappy open when the baby let out a massive fart and a poo projectile. My Boyfriend thought he was being clever

and dodged out of the way, but it went all over our new carpet and he had to spend ages cleaning it up! He is now very careful when nappy changing as he knows what could happen!
Erica, USA

I was once changing my Son in his Nursery, sat on his rocking chair. I had everything I needed ready. He had dirtied his nappy so I took it off and cleaned him up. As I was about to reach for his nappy he decided to be sick so I reached for a muslin to clean him up and then reached for his nappy (which was on the floor so I had to lean over him to get it). As soon as my face was next to his bottom he let out a massive trump and out came more poo with it, and it went all over my face and hair! Then he did a wee and soaked me with that! I didn't know where to start with the cleaning up and just sat there in shock for about five minutes!
Alicia, UK

I was changing my little girl's nappy a month or so ago, and she had a tummy bug and diarrhea. I was just applying some nappy rash cream when she decided to do a projectile poo! It shot across the room and landed in my Husband's glass of wine!
Erica, UK

My little boy has a thing about pooing when he is in the bath. My Husband bathed him the other night and would not listen to me when I warned him not to get in with him. He was at the stage when his poo was all yellow and

sticky and you guessed it, he pooed. The problem was that my Husband is very hairy and so the poo didn't just go in the water, it floated around and stuck to all his hair! He had to shout me to come and help with my Son while he had a shower! Next time maybe he will listen to me! Ha Ha!
Tricia, UK

My Husband, although our little one is now 6 months old, still comes running to me holding the baby out in front of him going "He's stinky! He's all yours!" While the poor baby hangs there naked from the waist down covered in poop. I say to him now "Yes dear, I can see that he's stinky, you really didn't need to bring him in here to show me!" Urgh Men!
Samantha, USA

When my little one was tiny my Mum was changing her bum when she farted and then poo shot out in a long line and wrapped itself around her arm about three times it was so funny! I couldn't help as I was laughing so much and my poor Mum didn't know what to say apart from "You never did that when you were little." Ha Ha!
Cheryl, UK

I was changing my baby on the mat and had just took the old nappy off. He started to pee and managed to pee in his own face, all down his cheek, in his ear and in his eye. He looked so surprised. I laughed because of his expression and then felt guilty for laughing, but would see

his face again and start laughing again, poor baby!
Diane, UK

I went with my Fiancé to the Mother in Law's for Sunday
dinner when our Son was around eight months old and he
needed changing. I was about to do it when Mother in
Law asked if she could change him so, glad of the offer, I
gave her the change bag. She had looked after him before
so she knew where everything was. My Son was playing
about ten minutes later when I noticed his pants were
wet so I went to change him again, not understanding
why as he had only just been changed. When I took his
jeans off I noticed that MIL had put his nappy on
backwards and his little willy was poking out! So as soon
as he peed it went straight through his clothes! She must
have been distracted and I thought it was best just not to
mention it! She never did it again though!
Janine, UK

My Daughter used to throw up a lot due to reflux. Once
she threw up all down me just as we were about to enter
a supermarket, I was so fed up I just cleaned it up the best
I could and went shopping! When we were at my Mother
in Law's, my Daughter projectile vomited across the room
and splashed my Mother in Law who was a good few feet
away from her, and got it in all the drinks in the way!
She is often terrified of men, but rather than just cuddling
me and ignoring them, she will scream hysterically, then
will calm again. She will turn to stare at them and then
start screaming again! I always feel so bad for them. A
lovely old man once left the bank we were in as he was so
embarrassed thinking he'd scared her.

Oh and she can clear a room of family in 5 seconds by pulling my top down for a feed!
Natalie, UK

A few weeks ago I went to Walmart to buy a Nintendo DS. I baby wore my Daughter so that I could be hands free. Well the cashier was extremely cute so I decided to flirt a little bit with him. I asked him if he would recommend the DS and if he could show it to me and laughed at some of the jokes he was saying. Just as he turned around to grab something my Daughter started to poop! It was super loud and very stinky! The guy grabbed what he needed and turned around and all we could hear was my Daughter's poop that basically sounded like adult diarrhea! I went super red and had to apologize for her smelly loud poop and just had to clarify that it wasn't me farting, because it kinda sounded like it!
I definitely hightailed it out of there without looking back!
Maria, USA

I was changing my Son's pee diaper, but while I was doing so he started pooping. Sadly, that wasn't the worst thing that happened. When I was wiping him I got some on my hand, but didn't notice. I felt an itch on my forehead and nose and scratched. I'm sure you can figure out what happened. I only noticed I had done this when I couldn't stop smelling poop!
Ellie, USA

My little boy was clinging onto my leg doing this little bounce that he does and going "Up, up up!" So I picked him up but at the same time kind of threw him into the air. He then threw up straight into my eye!

I was laughing, so was my Boyfriend. Instead of passing me a baby wipe to clean it he came and took a picture while I was blind in one eye! I could laugh about it afterwards!

When he was about three months old, we were queuing in a shop to buy some baby clothes, we were near the front and it was around Christmas time so the queue was huge. There was a Lady behind us and she was leaning into his pram cooing over him, he was smiling and doing little giggly noises at her, then all of a sudden he did the loudest and smelliest poo ever! I was so embarrassed and I think the lady was too! She didn't say anything, kind of just backed away as much as she could. The smell was so bad and there was no escape Ha Ha! Luckily there was only two people in front of me by this time so I got served pretty quickly and left!

Debbie, UK

The other day my sixteen month old was playing in the living room, just wearing her nappy while I was feeding her little Brother. She did a poo and it leaked out one of the sides of her nappy and I hadn't noticed as it wasn't that smelly. I only realised she'd done a poo when I saw little poo coloured lines all over my cream living room carpet from where she'd sat down! Yuck!

Cheryl, UK

My Sister in Law was holding my two week old little girl for a picture with all the kids at her wedding. She did her 'I'm going to poo' face so I ran and grabbed her as she had a tendency to shoot it up her back (it was summer so she had no vest on). As I took her from her she tilted back a little and a big blob of runny poo fell out onto my 3 year old Nieces white bridesmaid dress!

Thank god it was that early breastfeeding poo that's easily cleaned off!

Julie, UK

We went to my Sister in Law's house for my little one's first birthday. We gave all the kids a bath together, Nephew age 6, Niece age 4, and my Son, age 1. My Son stood up and was kind of jumping around and splashing and the next thing I know I hear my Nephew screaming and jumping out of the bath saying "Eww, eww, eww!" My Sister in Law asked him what was wrong, just as I saw my Son had a huge grown-up type poo sticking out of his bottom. I tried to pick my Son up and get him to the toilet before it dropped out, but as soon as I picked him up it dropped onto my Niece's lap at which point she let out the world's loudest scream! Also because everyone was freaking out and screaming it scared my happy go lucky Son and he started bawling as well. I felt so bad for all of them, my Son had never pooed in the bath before in his life so if I thought it was a big risk I wouldn't have bathed them all together. Needless to say my Niece and Nephew are not In any hurry to bath with my little one again!

Freya, UK

My Daughter was about two weeks old and my Mother had just fed her, so I asked her if she need a diaper change. My Mother moved my Daughter up to her eye level and peeked in the side of her diaper but before she

could close the diaper my Daughter farted so loud I could hear it across the room. It was so funny and my Mother's face turned bright red and she laughed. My Daughter still remains the only grandchild who has farted in her face!
Nicole, USA

When my Son was just a few days old, and my Mom was staying with us to help out, I lay him down to change his diaper and just about the time I took off the dirty one, he was sick, and I panicked and picked him up. Just as I did he had a really powerful poop and it shot all over our bed! I just didn't know what to do, I went to set him down, then I picked him back up, and went to set him down again and it wound up looking like I was trying to do aerobics with him! My mom saw me and just calmly came over and took him and said "Let's just finish him and then clean the bed." I was really grateful she was there.
Shauna, USA

I was out of the house one day, and I guess we must have ran out of diapers because when I got home, my Husband had made one out of a maxi-pad, a dish towel, and the headband I use when I take off my make-up! It worked, but now I make sure that I'm never, *ever* out of diapers!
Men!
Amy, USA

My Son was only about four days old when I got up from a nap and found that his Dad had taken the nasal bulb syringe that they give you at the hospital and given it to the baby to use as a pacifier. After I explained what it was,

he looked a little sheepish before saying "Good thing I rinsed it off first."
Mel, USA

Siblings and other Children:-

If you read my previous book then you will have read all the hilarious comments from siblings about their little Brother or Sister to be, but when the baby actually arrives, the situation changes and makes way for even more funny comments:-

We had to take our six month old to an emergency appointment at the Hospital recently and on our travels our three year old asked if we're going to collect a new baby. Then when I reminded him his new baby Brother is already here he casually asked "Can we not swap him?" Of course I said No!
Frankie, UK

My three year old Nephew says some cute things. When his little Brother was born I was watching both of them and the baby started to cry so my Nephew said "Well he's probably just hungry."

I said "Yeah you're right, but he'll be ok until Mommy gets back, she'll be here in a couple of minutes."
He said "Oh no, it's ok, you've got boobs so you can feed him." I just about died laughing, then told him that only Mommies can feed their baby!
Sarah, USA

My five year old Son knows babies have milk from Mummy's boobies but he cracked me up the other day when he asked "Where are the straws for the baby to get the milk out of?"
Erin, UK

When my Son was born, I breastfed him. On one of the mornings that I got to lay in bed and feed him my Daughter came into the room, cocked her head sideways and said, "Mommy, why brudder eat you boob?" After I had explained, she 'breastfed' all her baby dolls!
Sherri, South Dakota, USA

When my Son was a few months old my Mum was round visiting and I nipped to the shops. He started getting hungry just before I got home so Mum was comforting him (as he was breastfed). My eldest Daughter who was three at the time said, "Grandma, you've got boobies, why don't you just feed him?" I had to explain that one when I got home!
Anna, UK

My Nephew was watching his Mom breastfeeding his new baby Sister. After watching for a while and looking very confused, he asked: "Mom why have you got two? Is one for hot milk and one for cold milk?"
Me and my Sister couldn't stop laughing!
Donna, UK

I was breastfeeding my Daughter when she about five days old and my four year old Son wanted me to play. I said "I can't, I'm feeding the baby." So he went to the fridge and got our milk out and said "Here Mummy, just give her some of this." I didn't find it funny at the time, but everyone else did!
Belinda, UK

I remember when I brought my second Daughter home from the Hospital, my eldest Daughter was just over two and a half. I was holding the baby, and she said, "You always hold that baby, put it down!"
When I explained to her that Mummy had to hold the baby to feed her she looked at me and said (very seriously) "Well I think it's time for that baby to go back then."
On another occasion she was asked by a friend of mine how she liked having a baby Sister, to which she replied "Not much, all she does is cry!" Ha Ha!
Gloria, UK

I was at Kindergarten with my nearly four year old Daughter and my eight month old Son. I was sitting breastfeeding my Son when another child came up to me and asked "What you doing?"

I replied "I'm feeding my baby."

"Oh" he said and went out to play. After I had finished breastfeeding, my Son enjoyed a can of egg custard. I cleaned him up and popped him into the pushchair. The same Boy from earlier returned and asked "What did you feed your baby?"

I replied, "First milk, then egg custard." He stood, obviously in deep thought, for a few seconds and then asked "Which booby was the egg custard in?" I laughed until I cried!

Jenna, USA

My eldest Daughter is eight years old and one day I was cooking dinner and my three month old started fussing. I asked my eight year old to hold her for me until I finished. She was standing in the kitchen with me holding the baby. She looked at me and said, "Mommy, I wish the baby was a magnet so I could just stick her to the refrigerator." It took me a while to recover after laughing so much!

Alison, USA

When my Son was two I was playing with his Sister who was probably about four weeks old or so. My Son came up to me with a very annoyed look on his face and said, "No, Mama! Amy is *my* Sister. Your Sister is Emma. Go play with her so Amy can play with me."

Annabel, USA

I was in the waiting room at the Doctors and reading my two year old Son 'Hansel and Gretel' and we were chatting about the pictures etc. We got to the page where the scary old Witch is luring them inside. He pointed to her and yelled "Gramma!" I couldn't stop laughing! The people in the Doctor's office thought it was quite humorous too.
Abby, USA

My three year old Daughter was standing outside with my Mom and my neighbor, chatting away. My Daughter was playing happily in the grass when my neighbor's girlfriend asked for a corkscrew to open her wine bottle. I told her that I actually don't drink wine so I don't own a corkscrew. My Daughter promptly spoke up and said "My Gramma gots one cause she's a wino!" Dear me, where do they come up with this stuff? I certainly never said it to her!
Elizabeth, USA

I'm a breastfeeding Mum and feed in front of my toddler. The other day she was feeding her teddy and she shouted at the teddy "No bite!" and sent him to the naughty corner! I suppose I didn't realise how much she was taking in until I saw her copying!
Maddie, UK

My Son saw my Sister breastfeeding my Niece and asked my Sister what she was doing. My Sister calmly said that the baby was eating. My Son got a very concerned look on his face and asked "She's eating you?" He then came to me and said "Mom! baby's eating Auntie under her shirt!"

I said, "What?"

He said, "Baby is eating Auntie!" I then had to explain that babies eat *from* their Mommies, they don't actually eat them, and that my Sister was going to be okay!

Ruby, USA

One night after my youngest was born, we were all out to dinner. I noticed he was getting hungry so I handed him to my Mom so I could run to the ladies room. He started crying and my eldest asked "What's wrong?" Mom told him that the baby was hungry, so he lifted my Mom's shirt while saying "'So feed him, you have big boobies!" She told him that her 'boobies' didn't have milk in them. He ran to the bathroom and told me "Your Mother is rude and hates the baby! She refuses to share her boobs!" We tried to explain but he didn't get it. Poor guy was upset with her for over a month and kept saying how rude she was! Ha Ha!

Jennifer, USA

A few weeks had passed since I had my Daughter and I was outside the School gates, dropping my five year old Son off, and in front of all the other Mums he asked (very loudly) "Mummy, do those ladies all have jelly bellies because they've had babies?" I wanted the floor to swallow me up!

Kirsty, UK

I was out shopping with my four year old Daughter while my Husband was home with my baby boy. We had finished and were stood in quite a long queue at the

checkout, when my Daughter started chatting to an old Man behind us. She casually told him (and the rest of the shop) that her baby Brother was at home with Daddy. I thought this was quite sweet until she continued by saying "He came out of my Mummy's vagina. It had to stretch really big" (she outstretched her arms to show how big). I was mortified, especially when I saw the look of shock on the old Man's face. My Daughter finished by saying (with a big grin on her face) "It's ok though, because it stretched back again." The old Man just nodded and I could hear the stifled giggles from the other people who had overheard. I turned a shade of red I don't think I've been before!
Nadia, UK

My Son told me he was playing 'Mummies and Daddies' at School when the baby started crying. The Mummy said "Oh no, why is the baby crying?" My Son said "It just wants boobies." He has a baby Sister and is used to the baby crying! Ha Ha!
Caroline, UK

When my Son was about 3 weeks old, my Daughter had been ever so excited about helping Mummy feed the baby before he arrived and didn't really understand when I said "Only Mummy can feed him at first because he has 'booby milk' but when he has bottles you can help." When she questioned why she couldn't yet I explained she didn't have boobies yet as she was too little. Anyway, the baby was due for a feed one day and got to crying stage on my Husband's chest before I got to him. I nearly wet myself when my Daughter said very seriously "Don't

cry baby, Daddy will give you some milk from his boobies in a minute and then you won't be hungry." I had to explain that only Mummies boobies give milk. After that my Husband went on a diet to get rid of the 'moobs' ha ha!
Nicola, UK

When I was pregnant with my youngest I asked my Daughter (who was 6) if she wanted a Sister or a Brother. She said "What I want is a monkey." After her little Sister was born and was crying one day, my older Daughter said "See, I told you we should get a monkey."
Maria, USA

First words:-

Our baby's first word is eagerly awaited for such a long time but when it finally arrives, it can be rather surprising:-

Our youngest Son's first words were "Let go."' My Husband and I were puzzled buy this until we walked into a room one day to find his older Brothers playing tug-of-war with his favourite 'blankie.' In a tiny voice he stood his ground, yelling, "Let go, let go!"'
Laura, USA

My Husband was feeling down about the possibility of missing our Son's first word as he isn't around him as much as I am because of work. One morning, when he was leaving for work, he told our Son "I'll see you later, okay?" Smiling widely, our Son replied "Okay!"
Monica, USA

My Husband is always forgetting to take out the garbage and I have to remind him constantly about it. One morning, in the midst of my daily reminder, our nine month old, who was sitting in her high chair, looked straight at her Father, banged her fist, and yelled "Garbage out!" Stunned by those unusual first words, we both had a hearty laugh!
Sylvia, USA

I had practiced saying 'Momma' with our fourteen month old Daughter for weeks, acutely aware from her babbles that 'Dada' was on the way to becoming her first word. But both my Husband and I were unprepared for the day our baby uttered "Bob" as her first word, and sure enough, Bob (our golden retriever), came running to her call!
Sasha, USA

My Husband teases me mercilessly because I always say "Cool." One day, while feeding our baby, I asked him "Was that good?" To my surprise, he replied "Cool." We couldn't believe it!
Stephanie, USA

My Husband never thought the baby would say his name first, since I spent every day with her. But one morning, while he was in the shower, our Daughter yelled "Dada!" Elated, my Husband ran out of the bathroom dripping wet with nothing on but shaving cream and a huge grin!
Anne, USA

I was sitting in the Doctor's office with my 18 month old and I gave him a tongue stick to play with to keep him distracted. All of a sudden he shoved it down my top and said clear as day "cleavage." I just wanted the floor to swallow me up, of all the words to say! I still don't know where he got it from!
Samia, UK

Other incidents:-

Some funny things happen which are unrelated to any of the previous topics, but they still make us laugh, eventually!

I took my 6 month old Daughter on holiday last year. I had her in the carrier and was walking around a store. As I left the store the alarm went off! It turned out, as I was leaning over the shelves my baby had grabbed a twin pack of mini pork pies! She had them held tightly in her hand and I never noticed! Luckily we gave them back and didn't get done for shop lifting! Ha Ha.
Emily, UK

I was out shopping for the day and I'd just arrived at the retail park and my baby Son was whinging in the car. He always has a little moan just as he's about to fall asleep, but didn't have time to sleep before we got there so was in a foul mood when we arrived.
Very stupidly, I gave him my keys to keep him occupied while I struggled with the buggy. He looked at the keys,

and then very casually, tossed them over his shoulder. Not a problem ordinarily, but I'd locked the driver's door on my way out (force of habit) and the passenger door was still locked. I could see my keys on my handbrake but they were, well out of reach.

I had no other choice other than to empty everything out of the boot, get my Son out of his seat (through the boot!) and into his buggy, then climb through the boot to get into the car. So there I was, arse hanging out of the car, legs kicking away trying to pull myself through, dress hoiked up to my waist, knickers on display for everyone to see plus the fact that I'd parked in a Mum and Baby bay so it was right by the door of the store so lots of people got an eyeful. I got my keys, took my Son out of the buggy and put him back in the car then drove away as fast I could, shopping was cancelled!

Camilla, UK

I was at the Medical Centre, seeing the Nurse about my Daughter's eczema (she was 2 at the time). I was in mid-conversation and didn't notice what my Daughter was doing. The Nurse was typing away on her computer and then it just went black. I looked around and saw my Daughter with the computer's plug in her hand which she had just pulled out of the wall. She was very pleased with herself but the Nurse was not impressed and we had to wait ages for her computer to re-boot and for her to start again. It was the longest and most awkward time, I couldn't wait to get out of there!

Jess, UK

My Husband was sitting in the garden with our one year old Daughter. She was very into feeding everyone

whatever she was eating and she leaned over to my Husband and he wasn't really paying attention. She put something in his mouth and a few seconds later he jumped up, spitting something out. It was a dead fly! He now checks everything she 'feeds' him, just in case!
Charlotte, UK

That's all for this book, I hope you enjoyed reading! There are two more books in the 'Laugh Out Loud!' series:-

Laugh Out Loud! – Babies
Laugh Out Loud! – Kids

If you are leaving a review, thank you for your feedback! (you can write a review on the Amazon site or on goodreads)

You can find the Laugh Out Loud! Blog at http://laughoutloud-books.blogspot.co.uk/ where I am constantly adding new stories from my own family, especially comments from my little boy who makes me laugh every day!

I have also got a Facebook page dedicated to this series where you can add your own comments and stories at https://www.facebook.com/pages/Laugh-Out-Loud/420362314743645

Happy reading!   Sharon Irish

www.ingramcontent.com/pod-product-compliance
Lightning Source LLC
Chambersburg PA
CBHW071845020426
42331CB00007B/1857